COMMON
SENTENCE STRUCTURE
MISTAKES
AT TOEFL®

Richard Lee, Ph.D.

COLUMBIA PRESS

To Nancy S. T. , Philip, T. L., and Christina K. L.

CONTENTS

INTRODUCTION

Columbia Common Sentence Structure Mistakes at TOEFL is compiled to help you learn the absolutely essential grammar testing points and avoid the most common mistakes at TOEFL to raise your score! It has twenty lessons with each one having the following outstanding features:

- ERROR EXAMPLES: show you what kinds of mistakes most often made at TOEFL and how to correct them;
- GRAMMAR GUIDES: teach you the grammar rules absolutely essential to raise your TOEFL score;
- PRACTICE TESTS: Use sample Sentence Correction and Sentence Completion questions to test your grammar power and readiness for the real TOEFL;
- ANSWER KEYS: provide answers and explanations to help you avoid the mistakes forever to score higher on the TOEFL!

Columbia Common Sentence Structure Mistakes at TOEFL is your grammar Bible! With the help of our fun and effective way to learn all the essential grammar testing points, you will be able to score higher on the TOEFL guaranteed!

CHAPTER ONE

FAULTY SUBJECT

-VERB AGREEMENT

LESSON 1

TESTING POINT: AGREEMENT

-MODIFIED SUBJECT AND VERB

ERROR EXAMPLE

WRONG: In Washington, DC, the FBI Scientific Crime Detection Laboratory, better known as the FBI Crime Lab facilities, officially open.

RIGHT: In Washington, DC, the FBI Scientific Crime Detection Laboratory, better known as the FBI Crime Lab facilities, officially opens.

GRAMMAR GUIDE

A sentence must have a subject and a verb. In all patterns, the subject and the verb must agree in person and in number. Never use a verb that agrees with the modifier of a subject instead of with a subject itself.

WRONG: Everyone who had the opportunity to work beside the President and his cabinet were impressed by his vivision and leadership.

RIGHT: Everyone who had the opportunity to work beside the President and his cabinet was impressed by his vivision and leadership.

WRONG: Either of these buses go past College Park.

RIGHT: Either of these buses goes past College Park.

PRACTICE TEST

Test 1. SENTENCE COMPLETION: Choose the CORRECT answer.

A lot of students, each with an iPhone in his or her hand, _____.

   A. was busy texting or reading on the skytrain

   B. were busy texting or reading on the skytrain

Test 2. SENTENCE CORRECTION: Choose the INCORRECT word or phrase and CORRECT it.

1. His knowledge of languages and international relations aid him in his work.

2. The facilities at the new research library, including an excellent microfilm file, is among the best in the country.

3. All trade between the two countries were suspended pending negotiation of a new agreement.

4. The production of different kinds of artificial materials are essential to the conservation of our natural resources.

5. Since the shipment of supplies for our experiments were delayed, we will have to reschedule our work.

ANSWER KEY

Test 1: B (students were)

Test 2:

1. His knowledge of languages and international relations aids him in his work.

2. The facilities at the new research library, including an excellent microfilm file, are among the best in the country.

3. All trade between the two countries was suspended pending negotiation of a new agreement.

4. The production of different kinds of artificial materials is essential to the conversation of our natural resources.

5. Since the shipment of supplies for our experiments was delayed, we will have to reschedule our work.

LESSON 2

TESTING POINT:

AGREEMENT-SUBJECT WITH ACCOMPANIMENT AND VERB

ERROR EXAMPLE

WRONG: The Hollywood actress, Mary Shelly, along with the likes of Jenny Middleton and Nancy Tea, were added to the best-dressed list of the New Fashion Magazine.

RIGHT: The Hollywood <u>actress</u>, Mary Shelly, along with the likes of Jenny Middleton and Nancy Tea, <u>was</u> added to the best-dressed list of the New Fashion Magazine.

GRAMMAR GUIDE

Remember that the subject and the verb of a sentence must agree in number and in person. Never use a verb that agrees with a phrase of accompaniment instead of with the subject itself.

WRONG: The teen beauty, having been accepted by both Harvard and Yale, were also offered a Port of Entry scholarship.

RIGHT: The teen <u>beauty</u>, having been accepted by both Harvard and Yale, <u>was</u> also offered a Port of Entry scholarship.

PRACTICE TEST

Test 1. SENTENCE COMPLETION: Choose the CORRECT answer.

The famous scientist, accompanied by his doctoral students, _____ in order to prove the new theory of biogenetics.

    A. have conducted thorough research
    B. has conducted thorough research

Test 2. SENTENCE CORRECTION: Choose the INCORRECT word or phrase and CORRECT it.

1. The guest of honor, along with his wife and two sons, were seated at the first table.

2. The ambassador, with his family and staff, invite you to

   a reception at the embassy on Tuesday afternoon at five

   o'clock.

3. Mary, accompanied by her brother on the piano, were very well received at the talent show.

4. Senator MacDonald, with his assistant and his press secretary,

   are scheduled to arrive in New York today.

5. Bruce Springsteen, accompanied by the E. Street Band, are appearing in concert at the Student Center on Saturday night.

ANSWER KEY

Test 1: B (<u>scientist</u> <u>has</u>)

Test 2:

1. <u>The guest of honor</u>, along with his wife and two sons, <u>was</u> seated at the first table.

2. <u>The ambassador,</u> with his family and staff, <u>invites</u> you to a reception at the embassy on Tuesday afternoon at five o'clock.

3. <u>Mary,</u> accompanied by her brother on the piano, <u>was</u> very well received at the talent show.

4. <u>Senator MacDonald</u>, with his assistant and his press secretary, <u>is</u> scheduled to arrive in New York today

5. <u>Bruce Springsteen</u>, accompanied by the E. Street Band, <u>is</u> appearing in concert at the Student Center on Saturday night.

LESSON 3

TESTING POINT: AGREEMENT

-SUBJECT WITH APPOSITIVE AND VERB

ERROR EXAMPLE

WRONG: The Emperor, father of ninety children, were living a very extravagant life.

RIGHT: The Emperor, father of ninety children, was living a very extravagant life.

GRAMMAR GUIDE

The subject and the verb in a sentence must agree in person and in number. An appositive is a word or phrase that follows a noun and defines it. It usually has a comma before it and a comma after it.

Remember: never use a verb that agrees with words in the appositive after a subject instead of with the subject itself.

WRONG: New York, the Big Apple, are the only place in the world where dreams come true.

RIGHT: New York, the Big Apple, is the only place in the world where dreams come true.

PRACTICE TEST

Test 1. SENTENCE COMPLETION: Choose the CORRECT answer.

Cupid, one of the ancient Roman Gods, _____.

    A. were a little winged child
    B. was represented as a little winged child.

Test 2. SENTENCE CORRECTION: Choose the INCORRECT word or phrase and CORRECT it.

1. The books, an English dictionary and a chemistry textbook,

   was on the bookshelf yesterday.

2. Three swimmers from our team, Paul, Edward, and Jim, is in

   competition for medals.

3. Several pets, two dogs and a cat, needs to be taken care

   of while we are gone.

4. The Empire State University, the largest of state-supported school,

   have more than 50,000 students on its main campus.

5. This recipe, an old family secret, are an especially

   important part of our holiday celebrations.

ANSWER KEY

Test 1: B (Cupid   was)

Test 2:

1. The books, an English dictionary and a chemistry textbook, were on the bookshelf yesterday.

2. Three swimmers from our team, Paul, Edward, and Jim, are in competition for medals.

3. Several pets, two dogs and a cat, need to be taken care of while we are gone.

4. The Empire State University, the largest of state-supported school, has more than 50,000 students on its main campus.

5. This recipe, an old family secret, is an especially important part of our holiday celebrations.

CHAPTER TWO

UNCLEAR PRONOUN

REFERENCE

LESSON 4

TESTING POINT: CHECK PRONOUN

REFERENCE FOR AGREEMENT

ERROR EXAMPLE

WRONG: And when it comes to fathering healthy children, older men, it turns out, are just as much at the mercy of its biological clocks as women.

RIGHT: And when it comes to fathering healthy children, older men, it turns out, are just as much at the mercy of their biological clocks as women.

GRAMMAR GUIDE

A pronoun must clearly refer to the noun or noun phrase for which it substitutes.Remember that every pronoun and possessive agrees with the noun or noun phrase it refers to in number and in person.

WRONG: Mary paid more attention to her dog than its baby girl.

RIGHT: Mary paid more attention to her dog than her baby girl.

WRONG:.The committee and their members all voted in his favor.

RIGHT: The committee and its members all voted in his

favor.

PRACTICE TEST

Test 1. SENTENCE COMPLETION: Choose the CORRECT answer.

Although the destruction that_____is often terrible, cyclones

benefit a much wider belt than they devastate.

    A. they cause

    B. it causes

Test 2. SENTENCE CORRECTION: Choose the INCORRECT word or phrase and CORRECT it.

1. Nobody should be judged by their appearance.
2. We must let all citizens know his rights and obligations in the society.

3. He is one of those people who always brag about himself.

4. The current world situation gives the rich country more opportunities than the poor countries.

5. The students are trying their best to help the classmates in need.

ANSWER KEY

Test 1: A (they   cyclones)

Test 2:

1. Nobody should be judged by his appearance.

2. We must let all citizens know their rights and obligations in the society.

3. He is one of those people who always brag about themselves.

4. The current world situation gives the rich countries more opportunities than the poor countries.

5. The students are trying their best to help their classmates in need.

CHAPTER THREE

SHIFT IN PERSPECTIVE

LESSON 5

TESTING POINT: SHIFT IN AGENCY:

AGREEMENT-IMPERSONAL PRONOUNS

ERROR EXAMPLE

WRONG: One only has to add certain code next to his name for the organization one would like to support.

RIGHT: One only has to add certain code next to one's name for the organization one would like to support.

GRAMMAR GUIDE

Remember that there must be agreement of impersonal pronouns in a sentence. In formal writing, it is imperative that you continue using the impersonal pronoun *one* throughout a sentence. Never use *you, your, they,* or *their* to refer to the impersonal pronoun *one.*

WRONG: If one is willing to work hard, sooner or later,

he will succeed in life.

RIGHT: If <u>one</u> is willing to work hard, sooner or later,

one will succeed in life.

PRACTICE TEST

Test 1. SENTENCE COMPLETION: Choose the CORRECT answer.

The more hemoglobin one has, the more oxygen is carried to_____cells.

  A. their
  B. one's

Test 2. SENTENCE CORRECTION: Choose the INCORRECT word or phrase and CORRECT it.

1. At a large university, one will almost always be able to

    find a friend who speaks your language.

2. If one knew the facts, you would not be so quick to

    criticize.

3. In order to graduate, one must present their thesis thirty

    days prior to the last day of classes.

4. Regardless of one's personal beliefs, you have the

    responsibility to report the facts as impartially as

    possible.

5. If one does not work hard, you cannot expect to succeed.

ANSWER KEY

Test 1: B (<u>one</u>...<u>one's</u>)

Test 2:

1. At a large university, <u>one</u> will almost always be able to find a friend who speaks <u>one's</u> language.

2. If <u>one</u> knew the facts, <u>one</u> would not be so quick to criticize.

3. In order to graduate, <u>one</u> must present <u>one's</u> thesis thirty days prior to the last day of classes.

4. Regardless of <u>one's</u> personal beliefs, <u>one</u> has the responsibility to report the facts as impartially as possible.

5. If <u>one</u> does not work hard, <u>one</u> cannot expect to succeed.

LESSON 6

TESTING POINT: SHIFT IN TENSE:

CHECK VERB TENSE MEANINGS

ERROR EXAMPLE

WRONG: In the weeks since the debt ceiling agreement was approved, it became increasingly clear that good government might be impossible in the US.

RIGHT: In the weeks <u>since</u> the debt ceiling agreement <u>was approved,</u> it <u>has become</u> increasingly clear that good government might be impossible in the US.

GRAMMAR GUIDE

The verb tense in a sentence must agree with the time meaning of the rest of the sentence. Remember that the time meaning of a sentence is often determined by words or expressions that act as time markers, such as *yesterday, last week, next year, since, during, for, already,* etc.

WRONG: Mary Jones said that she will come to my birthday party on Sunday.

RIGHT: Mary Jones <u>said</u> that she <u>would</u> come to my birthday party on Sunday.

PRACTICE TEST

Test 1. SENTENCE COMPLETION: Choose the CORRECT answer.

In 1992, Bi11 Clinton_____President of the United States, after he_____his opponent by a wide margin.

    A. became   had beaten
    B. has become...had beaten

Test 2. SENTENCE CORRECTION: Choose the INCORRECT word or phrase and CORRECT it.

1. By the time I got to the airport, the plane has already taken off.

2. I traveled to five major cities since I cam to America last year.

3. The ground is wet. It must rained.

4. I took a shower when Helen called me.

5. By 2009 I will finish my bachelor's degree in computer

ANSWER KEY

Test 1: A (<u>became</u> refers to the thing happened in the past, <u>had beaten</u> refers to the thing that had happened before the past)

Test 2:

1. By the time I got to the airport, the plane had already taken off.

2. I have traveled to five major cities since I cam to America last year.

3. The ground is wet. It must have rained.

4. I was taking a shower when Helen called me.

5. By 2009 I will have finished my bachelor's degree in computer science.

LESSON 7

TESTING POINT: SHIFT IN VOICE: CHECK PASSIVE AND ACTIVE SENTENCES

ERROR EXAMPLE

WRONG: If we can't agree by the end of the meeting, the matter will have to take a vote.

RIGHT: If we can't agree by the end of the meeting, a <u>vote</u> will <u>have to be taken</u> on the matter.

GRAMMAR GUIDE

Sentences in which the error is an incorrect passive are common in standardized tests. Therefore, you must be able to determine whether an active voice or a passive voice of the verb is needed in a sentence.

32

WRONG: If you want to be rich, a college education must be received nowadays.

RIGHT: If you want to be rich, <u>you must receive</u> a college education nowadays.

PRACTICE TEST

Test 1. SENTENCE COMPLETION: Choose the CORRECT answer.

The writer of this article_____great concern about the recession.

   A. has been expressed
   B. has expressed

Test 2. SENTENCE CORRECTION: Choose the INCORRECT word or phrase and CORRECT it.

1. The whole birthday cake was eaten by John.

2. Bob plays the piano and the guitar is played by him also.

3. The house was bought by my mother and father in 1980.

4. Most of these toys made in China.

5. He made to believe that he was adopted by his parents.

ANSWER KEY

Test 1: B (<u>has expressed</u>, the active voice is needed here)

Test 2:

1. John _ate_ the whole birthday cake.

2. Bob _plays the piano_ and also _the guitar_.

3. My _mother and father bought_ the house in 1980.

4. Most to these toys _were made_ in China.

5. He _was made_ to believe that he was adopted by his parents.

CHAPTER FOUR

FAULTY PARALLEL STRUCTURE

LESSON 8

TESTING POINT: USE PARALLEL STRUCTURE WITH COORDINATE CONJUNCTIONS

ERROR EXAMPLE

WRONG: Jimmy likes to go crab fishing during the day, but Justin prefers catching sharks at night.

RIGHT: Jimmy likes <u>to go</u> crab fishing during the day, but Justin prefers <u>to catch</u> sharks at night.

GRAMMAR GUIDE

Coordinate conjunctions (*and, but, or, yet, for, nor*) join together equal expressions. These conjunctions can join nouns, verbs, adjectives, phrases, subordinate clauses, and main clauses. Remember that they must join together two of the same thing.

WRONG: Peter Johnson is not a professor nor is he a lawyer.

RIGHT: Peter Johnson is not a professor nor a lawyer.

WRONG: I am not interested in what you are saying it but your doing it.

RIGHT: I am not interested in what you are saying it but how you are doing it.

PRACTICE TEST

Test 1. SENTENCE COMPLETION: Choose the CORRECT answer.

Nancy suggested taking the plane this evening or _____.

    A. going by train tomorrow
    B. that we go by train tomorrow

Test 2. SENTENCE CORRECTION: Choose the INCORRECT word or phrase and CORRECT it.

1. Jennifer thought it was essential that she succeed and skiing.

2. He love her dearly but not her cat.

3. Jake left his pet rabbit out in the cold and alone.

4. I wanted to go to the party, and Peter never intended to go.

5. Christine worked very hard, and she knew she would not keep her job if she did not.

ANSWER KEY

Test 1: A (taking   going…are of the same thing: gerunds.)

Test 2:

1. Jennifer thought it was essential <u>that she succeed</u> and <u>that she ski</u> regularly.

2. He <u>loved her</u> dearly but he <u>did not love her cat</u>.

3. Jake left his pet rabbit <u>out in the cold</u> and <u>by itself</u>.

4. I wanted to go to the party, <u>yet</u> Peter never intended to go.

5. Christine worked very hard, <u>for</u> she knew she would not keep her job if she did not.

LESSON 9

TESTING POINT: USE PARALLEL STRUCTURE WITH CORRELATIVE CONJUNCTIONS

ERROR EXAMPLE

WRONG: Reservation of a necessary portion of an estate shall be made in a will for a successor who neither can work or he has a source of income.

RIGHT: Reservation of a necessary portion of an estate shall be made in a will for a successor who <u>neither</u> can work <u>nor</u> has a source of income.

GRAMMAR GUIDE

The paired conjunctions *both… and, either… or, neither… nor,* and *not only… but also, whether…or* require parallel structures. These conjunctions can join nouns, verbs, adjectives, phrases, subordinate clauses, and main clauses.Remember that they must join together two of the same thing.

WRONG: He is not only an excellent student but also he is an

outstanding athlete.

RIGHT: He is not only <u>an excellent student</u> but also <u>an</u>

<u>outstanding athlete</u>.

WRONG: I know neither Spanish nor speaking French

.**RIGHT:** I know neither <u>Spanish</u> nor <u>French</u>.

PRACTICE TEST

Test 1. SENTENCE COMPLETION: Choose the CORRECT answer.

The new movie was neither amusing nor_____.

    A. was it interesting.
    B. interesting

Test 2. SENTENCE CORRECTION: Choose the INCORRECT word or phrase and CORRECT it.

1. He is neither well qualified or sufficiently experienced for that position.

2. That horse is not only the youngest one in the race and the only one to win two years in a row.

3. Neither the public or the private sector of the economy will be seriously affected by this regulation.

4. He refused to work either in Chicago nor in Vancouver.

5. Mary decided not only to start a diet, but to join a fitness club.

ANSWER KEY

Test 1: B (amusing...interesting...are of the same thing: adjectives)

Test 2:

1. He is neither well qualified nor sufficiently experienced for that position.

2. That horse is not only the youngest one in the race but also the only one to win two years in a row.

3. Neither the public nor the private sector of the economy will be seriously affected by this regulation.

4. He refused to work either in Chicago or in Vancouver.

5. Mary decided not only to start a diet, but also to join a fitness club.

CHAPTER FIVE

FAULTY SUBJECT/

DANGLING MODIFIER

LESSON 10

TESTING POINT: DANGLING PARTICIPLE: CHECK -*ING* AND -*ED* MODIFYING PHRASES

ERROR EXAMPLE

WRONG: Having won the world championship for swimming, the Chairman of the Olympic Committee presented the gold medal to the player.

RIGHT: Having won the world championship for swimming, the player was presented with a gold medal by the Chairman of the Olympic Committee.

GRAMMAR GUIDE

In English, -*ing* and-*ed* participles are used in phrases which modify the main clause. This structure, also known as a dangling modifier or dangling participle, is usually a –*ing* participial phrase or an –*ed*

43

participial phrase. The key to avoid this kind of mistake is that the doer of the action in both the dangling participle and the main clause must be the same person. For example:

WRONG: Having finished our class, it was time for us to go home.

RIGHT: Having <u>finished</u> our class, <u>we thought</u> it was time to go home.

PRACTICE TEST

Test 1. SENTENCE COMPLETION: Choose the CORRECT answer.

The squirrel, _____, hid its nuts in a variety of places.

   A. tried to prepare for winter

   B. trying to prepare for winter

Test 2. SENTENCE CORRECTION: Choose the INCORRECT word or phrase and CORRECT it.

1. Having finished dinner, it was time to go to the movies.

2. Being left alone, it was very scary for me in a big house.

3. With its antlers weblike the feet of a duck, the North American moose is easy to identify.

4. Anyone interesting in the game can participate.

5. Seeing the business opportunity, a shopping mall was built here by George.

ANSWER KEY

Test 1: B (<u>trying to prepare</u>…<u>hid</u>，the performer of both actions is the squirrel)

Test 2:

1. Having finished dinner,<u> we thought</u> it was time to go to the movies.

2. Being left alone, <u>I felt</u> it was very scary in a big house.

3. With its antlers <u>webbed like </u>the feet of a duck, the North American moose is easy to identify.

4. Anyone <u>interested </u>in the game can participate.

5. Seeing the business opportunity, <u>George </u>built a shopping mall here.

CHAPTER SIX

INCORRECT PREDICATION

LESSON **11**

TESTING POINT: AGREEMENT—COLLECTIVE SUBJECT AND VERB

ERROR EXAMPLE

WRONG: Our staff are well versed in the network, understands trade and understands the rich experience in plastics machinery in Indonesia.

RIGHT: Our <u>staff</u> <u>is</u> well versed in the network, understands trade and understands the rich experience in plastics machinery in Indonesia.

GRAMMAR GUIDE

The following collective subjects agree with singular verbs:

audience   *faculty*   *police*   *variety*

47

band	*family*	*public*	*2, 3, 4, ...*
dollars	*chorus*	*group*	*series*
2, 3, 4, ...miles	*class*	*majority*	*staff*
committee	*orchestra*	*team*	

The following subject agrees with a plural verb:

people

Never use plural verbs with singular subjects nor do you use singular verbs with plural subjects.

WRONG: A good team result in both recruiting and coaching as well as performing.

RIGHT: A good team <u>is a result of</u> both recruiting and

coaching as well as performing.

PRACTICE TEST

Test 1. SENTENCE COMPLETION: Choose the CORRECT answer.

The Graduate Committee_____your application for admission into our MBA program for the Fall of 2012.

   A. has approved

   B. have approved

Test 2. SENTENCE CORRECTION: Choose the INCORRECT word or phrase and CORRECT it.

1. Twenty dollars are the price.

2. Many people is coming to the graduation.

3. An audience usually do not applaud in a church.

4. Four miles are the distance to the office.

5. The staff are meeting in the conference room.

ANSWER KEY

Test 1: A (<u>committee</u>   <u>has</u>)

Test 2:

1. Twenty dollars <u>is</u> the price.

2. Many people <u>are</u> coming to the graduation.

3. An audience usually <u>does not</u> applaud in a church.

4. Four miles <u>is</u> the distance to the office.

5. The staff <u>is</u> meeting in the conference room.

CHAPTER SEVEN

MISPLACED MODIFIER

LESSON 12

TESTING POINT:

POSITION ADJECTIVES

AND ADVERBS CORRECTLY

ERROR EXAMPLE

WRONG: He began hosting sporadically bug dinner parties, gatherings of friends and friends of friends.

RIGHT: He began <u>sporadically</u> hosting bug dinner parties, gatherings of friends and friends of friends.

GRAMMAR GUIDE

In English, an adjective normally appears in front of the noun it modifies. For adverbs, it can appear in many positions, however, it can not come in between a verb and its object.

WRONG: I have news important to tell you tonight.

RIGHT: I have <u>important news</u> to tell you tonight.

WRONG: Jennifer is studying very hard French with the help of a private tutor from Paris.

RIGHT: Jennifer <u>is studying</u> French <u>very hard</u> with the help of a private tutor from Paris.

PRACTICE TEST

Test 1. SENTENCE COMPLETION: Choose the CORRECT answer.

To share his expensive apartment downtown, Jacky_____.

   A. is desperately looking for a new roommate

   B. is looking for a new roommate desperately

Test 2. SENTENCE CORRECTION: Choose the INCORRECT word or phrase and CORRECT it.

1. I only have one best friend in New York City.

2. She has bought just a new four-door Ford.

3. We thought it was importantly something we had to do.

4. Michael has been late terrible for class recently.

5. Is there anything with your computer wrong?

ANSWER KEY

Test 1: A

Test 2:

1. I have only one best friend in New York City.

2. She has just bought a new four-door Ford.

3. We thought it was something important we had to do.

4. Michael has been terribly late for class recently.

5. Is there anything wrong with your computer?

CHAPTER EIGHT

PROBLEMS WITH CONJUNCTIONS

LESSON 13

TESTING POINT: USE

CONJUNCTIONS CORRECTLY

ERROR EXAMPLE

WRONG: The Chief Executive Officer said Apple told him some of the factories on his list were not the US company's suppliers and gave him no details.

RIGHT: The Chief Executive Officer said Apple told him some of the factories on his list were not the US company's suppliers <u>but</u> gave him no details.

GRAMMAR GUIDE

In English, conjunctions are connecting words; they join parts of a sentence. Coordinate conjunctions (*and, or, but, nor*) are used to join equal sentence parts: single words, phrases, and independent clauses. The conjunction *so* is used to join only clauses-not single words or phrases. When two full clauses are joined, they are usually separated by a comma.

Correlative conjunctions (*both...and, not only... but also, either or, neither nor*) are two-part conjunctions. Like coordinate conjunctions, they are used to join clauses, phrases, and words.

WRONG: Jackson is not only a famous movie star but a powerful
                politician.

RIGHT: Jackson is <u>not only</u> a famous movie star <u>but also</u> a powerful
                politician..

WRONG: Michael Joyce is one of the richest men in America and
                lives a very simple life.

RIGHT: Michael Joyce is one of the richest men in

                America <u>but</u> lives a very simple life.

PRACTICE TEST

Test 1. SENTENCE COMPLETION: Choose the CORRECT answer.

Neither the students_____were happy about the tuition increase in the state college system.

   A. or the parents

   B. nor the parents

Test 2. SENTENCE CORRECTION: Choose the INCORRECT word or phrase and CORRECT it.

1. The store does not only sell books but CD's and DVD's.

2. Jackson is the best student in the class and he failed the exam this time.

3..The Rockies are beautiful and supernatural.

4. This book includes only not records bust also cassettes.

5. Neither the public or the private sector of the economy will benefit from this new legislation.

ANSWER KEY

Test 1: B (neither…nor must be used together)

Test 2:

1. The store does <u>not only</u> sell books <u>but also</u> CD's and DVD's.

2. Jackson is the best student in the class <u>but</u> he failed the exam this time.

3. The Rocky Mountains are <u>both</u> beautiful <u>and</u> supernatural.

4. This book includes <u>not only</u> records <u>but also</u> cassettes.

5. <u>Neither</u> the public <u>nor</u> the private sector of the economy will benefit from this new legislation.

CHAPTER NINE

INCOMPLETE SENTENCE

LESSON 14

TESTING POINT: INCOMPLETE INDEPENDENT CLAUSES

ERROR EXAMPLE

WRONG: In the countryside of undeveloped countries, where people are still suffering from hunger and cold.

RIGHT: In the countryside of undeveloped countries, there are people still suffering from hunger and cold.

GRAMMAR GUIDE

All sentences consist of one or more clauses. a simple sentence consists of one clause. Each clause must have a subject and a verb.

WRONG: The famous song writer, there were a lot of beautiful songs.

RIGHT: The famous song writer wrote a lot of beautiful songs.

A compound sentence consists of two dependent clauses joined by a coordinating conjunction(such *as* and and *but*).

WRONG: With only a few of the sounds produced by

insects can be heard by humans.

RIGHT: Only a few of the <u>sounds</u> produced by insects

<u>can be heard</u> by humans.

A complex sentence consists of an independent clause (called the main clause) and a subordinate (dependent) clause. Subordinate clauses may be adverb clauses, noun clauses, or adjective clauses.

WRONG: Before the invention of the printing press, books that were very rare.

RIGHT: Before the invention of the printing press, <u>books were</u> very <u>rare</u>.

PRACTICE TEST

Test 1. SENTENCE COMPLETION: Choose the CORRECT answer.

Stephen King, the bestselling novelist, _____ for his horror stories.

  A. who became famous

  B. became famous

Test 2. SENTENCE CORRECTION: Choose the INCORRECT word or phrase and CORRECT it.

1. There takes five people to carry this huge box to the storage room.

2. The boy won the national spelling bee contest, and he failed his

grade test at School for all subjects.

3. Although he had only a college degree, but he got a professorship at a majorAmerican university.

4. Having a lot money not always a good thing for the young people.

5. In Beijing alone, have about sixteen million people.

ANSWER KEY

Test 1: B (<u>Stephen King</u>...<u>became famous</u>: King is the subject and became is the verb.)

Test 2:

1. <u>It takes</u> five people to carry this huge box to the storage room.

2. The boy won the national spelling bee contest,<u> but</u> he failed his grade test at School for all subjects.

3. <u>Although</u> he had only a college degree, he got a professorship at a major American university.

4. Having a lot of money<u> is </u>not always a good thing for the young people.

5. In Beijing alone, <u>there are</u> about twelve million people.

LESSON 15

TESTING POINT: INCOMPLETE

ADJECTIVE CLAUSES

ERROR EXAMPLE

WRONG: It could have been a simple mistake or misunderstanding, he surely wouldn't have been discharged.

RIGHT: It could have been a simple mistake or misunderstanding, <u>for which</u> he surely wouldn't have been discharged.

GRAMMAR GUIDE

Adjective clauses or relative clauses are a way of joining two sentences together into one sentence. In the joined sentence, the adjective clause modifies a noun or pronoun in the main clause. The adjective clause is introduced by relative pronouns (*who, whom, whose, that, which*) or relative adverbs (*when, where*).

WRONG: The melting point is the temperature which a

solid changes to a liquid.

RIGHT: The melting point is the temperature <u>at which</u> a solid changes to a liquid.

WRONG: In life, it is not who you are but who you are with.

RIGHT: In life, it is not who you are but <u>whom</u> you are with.

WRONG; This mountain village is the place the President of he United States was born.

RIGHT: This mountain village is the place <u>where</u> the

President of the United States was born.

PRACTICE TEST

Test 1. SENTENCE COMPLETION: Choose the CORRECT answer.

On the first day at school, I ran into Dr. Samuel Johnson, a distinguished Shakespearean scholar_____.

   A. who I have been looking forward to meeting with

   B. whom I have been looking forward to meeting with

Test 2. SENTENCE CORRECTION: Choose the INCORRECT word or phrase and CORRECT it.

1. He has five brothers who he loves with all his heart.

2. This is the place that Chairman Mao was born.

3. That he has won the big lottery really unbelievable.

4. We established the charity foundation gave scholarships to qualified

students.

5. How he got to Yale law school known to nobody.

ANSWER KEY

Test 1: B (scholar <u>whom</u>....<u>meet with</u>: here *whom* is the object of *with*)

Test 2:

1. He has five brothers <u>whom</u> he loves with all his heart.

2. This is the place <u>where</u> Chairman Mao was born.

3. That he has won the big lottery <u>is</u> really unbelievable.

4. We established the charity foundation <u>which</u> gave scholarships to qualified students.

5. How he got to Yale law school <u>is</u> known to nobody.

LESSON 16

TESTING POINT: INCOMPLETE

ADVERB CLAUSES

ERROR EXAMPLE

WRONG: But he also said he was more cautious about the promise of generics this time, biotech medicines were not easy to copy.

RIGHT: But he also said he was more cautious about the promise of generics this time, <u>because</u> biotech medicines were not easy to copy.

GRAMMAR GUIDE

An adverb clause consists of a connecting word, called an adverb clause marker (subordinate conjunctions like *because, since, although, even though, while, if, unless, when, as, until, once, before, after*), and it must have a subject and a verb.

An adverb clause can also be introduced by adverb clause markers like *however, wherever, whenever.*

WRONG: Liquid magma rises to the surface of the earth, a volcano is formed.

RIGHT: Whenever liquid magma rises to the surface of the earth, a volcano is formed.

WRONG: Despite they are tropical birds, parrots can live in temperate or even cold climates.

RIGHT: Even though they are tropical birds, parrots can live in temperate or even cold climates.

PRACTICE TEST

Test 1. SENTENCE COMPLETION: Choose the CORRECT answer.

Michael Douglas can not be the President of the Student Union_____.

   A. unless he apologizes for cheating on his exams.

   B. if he apologizes for cheating on his exams.

Test 2. SENTENCE CORRECTION: Choose the INCORRECT word or phrase and CORRECT it.

1. Despite he is good student, we can not offer him admission at this time.

2. Wherever go, you have to prove that you have enough funding for your visa.

3. Nobody can predict will happen because tomorrow is uncertain.

4. The train was late for two hours due the weather conditions in the Rockies.

5. Some students were singing when others were dancing.

ANSWER KEY

Test 1: A (<u>not</u>...<u>unless</u>: they must be used in pairs as double negation)

Test 2:

1. <u>Despite the fact that</u> he is a good student, we can not offer him admission at this time.

2. <u>Wherever you go</u>, you have to prove that you have enough funding for your visa.

3. Nobody can predict <u>what</u> will happen because tomorrow is uncertain.

4. The train was late for two hours <u>due to</u> the weather conditions in the Rockies.

5. Some students were singing <u>while</u> others were dancing.

CHAPTER TEN

FAULTY LOGICAL RELATIONS BETWEEN CLAUSES

LESSON 17

TESTING POINT: USE

ADVERB *TIME* AND *CAUSE*

MARKERS CORRECTLY

ERROR EXAMPLE

WRONG: The family suspects a hotel employee, she said, the thieves used a copy of their electronic key to get into their room.

RIGHT: The family suspects a hotel employee, she said, <u>since</u> the thieves used a copy of their electronic key to get into their room.

GRAMMAR GUIDE

An adverb clause consists of a connecting word, called an adverb clause marker.

The common adverb *time* markers are: *after, as soon as, once, when, as, before, since, whenever, as long as, by the time, until, while.*

The common adverb *cause* markers are: *as, now that, because, since, in as much as.*

Remember that an adverb clause must have a subject and a verb.

WRONG: The children had gone to sleep as I got home last night.

RIGHT: The children had gone to sleep <u>by the time</u> I got home last night.

WRONG: I was late for the appointment, I did not get the job.

RIGHT: <u>Because</u> I was late for the appointment, I did not get the job.

PRACTICE TEST

Test 1. SENTENCE COMPLETION: Choose the CORRECT answer.

_____, the farmers planted the seedlings carefully.

   A. The ground had been prepared.

   B. After the ground had been prepared

Test 2. SENTENCE CORRECTION: Choose the INCORRECT word or phrase and CORRECT it.

1. Tom didn't practice driving, and he failed his road test..

2. They got to the railway station and the train had already left.

3. The graduation party didn't begin as all the students arrive.

4. I have made quite a few friends when I cam to New York City.

5. Maple wrote our new business plan while I did the local market research..

ANSWER KEY

Test 1: B (<u>after</u> ...<u>had been prepared</u>...<u>planted:</u> here the adverbial clause of time is introduced by *after,* there is a logical sequence of time involved.)

Test 2:

1. <u>Because</u> Tom didn't practice driving, he failed his road test.

2. <u>By the time</u> they got to the railway station, the train had already left.

3. The graduation party did not begin <u>until </u>all the students arrive.

4. I have made quite a few friends<u> since </u>I cam to New York City.

5. Maple wrote our new business plan, <u>and</u> I did the local market research.

LESSON 18

TESTING POINT: USE

ADVERB *CONTRAST, CONDITION,*

MANNER, AND *PLACE* MARKERS

CORRECTLY

ERROR EXAMPLE

WRONG: Chanel could run miles in her younger days, now she suffers from joint problems and spends most of her days at home.

RIGHT: Although Chanel could run miles in her younger days, now she suffers from joint problems and spends most of her days at home.

GRAMMAR GUIDE

An adverb clause consists of a connecting word, called an adverb clause marker.

The common adverb *contrast* markers are: *although, even though, though, while, whereas*

The common adverb *condition* markers are: *if, in case, provided, providing, unless, whether.*

The adverb *manner* markers are: *as, in that.*

The adverb *place* markers are: *where, wherever.*

Remember that an adverb clause must have a subject and a verb.

WRONG: You will go to Beijing with us for the summer providing you pass the state test.

RIGHT: You will go to Beijing with us for the summer <u>provided</u> you pass the state test.

WRONG: Mr. Nicolson is not very rich, he is always willing to help those in need.

RIGHT: <u>Even though</u> Mr. Nicolson is not very rich, he is always willing to help those in need.

PRACTICE TEST

Test 1. SENTENCE COMPLETION: Choose the CORRECT answer.

No one can be admitted into the Board of Directors _____.

   A. if he has the required qualifications

   B. unless he has the required qualifications

Test 2. SENTENCE CORRECTION: Choose the INCORRECT word or phrase and CORRECT it.

1. A good time is where time goes by quickly.

2. I will go with you unless you drive.

3. As you want less noise, you can move to the country.

4. President Kennedy committed the U.S. to being the first to land on the moon, and he died before he saw his dream realized.

5. We read in the newspaper where they are making great progress in DNA research in China.

ANSWER KEY

Test 1: B (no one…unless)

Test 2:

1. A good time is when time goes by quicky.

2. I will go with you provided that you drive.

3. If you want less noise, you can move to the country.

4. President Kennedy committed the U.S. to being the first to land on the moon, but he died before he saw his dream realized.

5. We read in the newspaper that they are making great progress in DNA research in China.

LESSON **19**

TESTING POINT:

LOGICAL CONSTRUCTIONS

-EVENTS IN THE PAST

ERROR EXAMPLE

WRONG: Mary had high fever last night, she caught a very bad cold on her way home.

RIGHT: Mary had high fever last night, she <u>must have caught</u> a very bad cold on her way home.

GRAMMAR GUIDE

Remember that *must* is a modal verb. When *must* is

followed by auxiliary verb *have* + past participle, it

expresses a logical conclusion based on evidence. The

conclusion is about an event happened in the past.

WRONG: When the weather becomes colder, we know that the air mass is originated in the Arctic rather than over the Gulf of Mexico.

RIGHT: When the weather becomes colder, we know that the air mass must <u>have originated</u> in the Arctic rather than over the Gulf of Mexico.

PRACTICE TEST

Test 1. SENTENCE COMPLETION: Choose the CORRECT answer.

Being on the list of 400 richest Americans, Douglas Cabinsky, the car dealer_____.

   A. must work very hard

   B. must have worked very hard.

Test 2. SENTENCE CORRECTION: Choose the INCORRECT word or phrase and CORRECT it.

1. The streets are wet; it should have rained last night.

2. This pen won't write; it can have run out of ink (in the past).

3. The ring that I was looking at is gone; someone else must buy it.

4. He doesn't have his keys; he must locked them in his car.

5. I don't see Martha any where; she must be left early.

ANSWER KEY

Test 1: B (being on…must have worked: logical conclusion based on evidence)

Test 2:

1. The streets are wet; it must have rained last night.

2. This pen won't write; it must have run out of ink (in the past).

3. The ring that I was looking at is gone; someone else must have bought it.

4. He doesn't have his keys; he must have locked them in his car.

5. I don't see Martha any where; she must have left early.

LESSON **20**

TESTING POINT: LOGICAL CONCLUSIONS –EVENTS IN THE PRESENT

ERROR EXAMPLE

WRONG: Me: "Fine, but I didn't pay the last time. They must do things differently down in the south."

RIGHT: Me: "Fine, but I didn't pay the last time. They <u>must be doing</u> things differently down in the south."

GRAMMAR GUIDE

Remember that *must* is a modal verb. When *must* is

followed by auxiliary verb *have* + be + *ing* or an adjective, it

expresses a logical conclusion based on evidence. The

conclusion is about an event happening now. Remember

that avoid using a verb in its original form instead of the

-*ing* form.

WRONG: The rich people must buy a lot of expensive cars now because the prices are going up.

RIGHT: The rich people <u>must be buying</u> a lot of expensive cars now because the prices are going up.

PRACTICE TEST

Test 1. SENTENCE COMPLETION: Choose the CORRECT answer.

Since the American buffalo has been removed from the endangered species list, it_____itself again.

   A. must reproduce

   B. must be reproducing

Test 2. SENTENCE CORRECTION: Choose the INCORRECT word or phrase and CORRECT it.

1. The line is busy; someone should be using the telephone now.

2. Bob is absent; he must have been sick again (now).

3. He is taking a walk; he must have felt better now.

4. She must be study at the library now because all of her books are gone.

5. Sarah must get a divorce (now) because her husband is living in an apartment.

ANSWER KEY

Test 1: B (since…has been removed…must be reproducing: logical conclusion based on evidence)

Test 2:

1. The line is busy; someone must be using the telephone now.

2. Bob is absent; he must be sick again (now).

3. He is taking a walk; he must be feeing better now.

4. She must be studying at the library now because all of her books are gone.

5. Sarah must be getting a divorce (now) because her husband is living in an apartment.

Acknowledgements

The author would like to thank his colleagues and students for bringing some of these mistakes to life.

The author and publisher are grateful to those who have made this publication possible by providing all kinds of support from editing, graphic design, and proof-reading. Efforts have been made to identify the source of materials used in this book, however, it has not always been possible to identify the sources of all the materials used, or to trace the copyright holders. If any omissions are brought to our attention, we will be happy to include the appropriate aknowlegements on reprinting.

ABOUT THE AUTHOR

Dr. Richard Lee is a professor of English and distinguished publishing scholar with more than ten books published under his name. His books are available on Amazon, other online stores, and in bookstores worldwide. Dr. Lee pursued his graduate education at the University of Rochester and the University of British Columbia and got his Ph.D. in English. He lives in beautiful Vancouver, British Columbia.

Printed in Great Britain
by Amazon

30313095R00050